NED

A Fish Tale written and illustrated by Patti Gibbons

The ocean is one of the most beautiful parts of planet Earth, and we are destroying it every day. Trash and waste are killing fish and reefs. Overfishing is causing entire species to disappear. It is not just the fish we catch, but the fish that depend on those caught fish for their food. Shark poaching and illegal harvesting are also big problems.

And so, this is a fish tale from Ned's point of view. I hope you enjoy it, but most of all, I hope it makes you think before you toss a bottle or plastic bag in the ocean or leave your trash on the beach.

This is Ned

Ned is of the genus Flatfishious Emotionalus, a species of fish that usually looks like any other fish. However, when this particular species feels any strong emotion, it blows up completely round AND completely flat. Alas, Ned is always hugely round AND flat because he is always full of strong emotions. But we'll get to that later.

Ned lives on a pristine reef in a tiny sea so remote that no scientist has ever charted its location, nor has any human being ever sailed upon or swam in its crystal blue waters.

Ned is a teacher of Reef Ecology. He earnestly and with great pride teaches his school of fish to respect their beautiful reef home and to swim thoughtfully throughout its sea life and plants. This reef will be the home of generations of sea life to come. Ned has never seen any reef but his own. However, many fish have passed through Ned's reef with frightening stories of faraway reefs that have been harmed beyond repair by creatures called human beings.

Now, this lovely fish is named Ophelia, of the species Princessia Spoiledalotta. She, too, inhabits Ned's reef and is the reason for Ned's dilemma; that strong emotion he feels all the time is his deep love for Ophelia. For Ned, Ophelia is the perfect fish.

CORAL
MALL

Ophelia doesn't know Ned exists. She spends most of her time swimming through the Coral Mall and hanging out with her friends at the Seaweed Ice Cream Shoppe. For Ophelia, it's like that Fish Song Classic, "Life is just a Bowl of Cherrystones" (made famous by The Reel Swim Shady, who, rumor has it, is back). Anyhow, Ophelia has her fish eyes on somebody besides Ned.

And this, my friends, is Barry Cuda, from no particular genus of fish. Most people can see right through him – probably because he's transparent! – but fish like Ophelia are distracted by his shiny pompadour, sparkling fins, and toothy smile. Rest assured that Barry is not a nice fish underneath the glimmer and the shimmer.

While Ned is focusing his attention on his students (and trying not to think about Ophelia too much), Ophelia is dreaming about becoming Ophelia Cuda, and Barry Cuda is up to no good. It seems he is swimming around with a particularly fishy bunch – a gang of sharks who call themselves "The Sharks," which speaks volumes about their level of intelligence and imagination. The Sharks are known for terrorizing their reef's inhabitants, as well as cruising outlying waters to confront those they think are ripe for bullying. But don't blame The Sharks – they have been persecuted for a very long time, and it has made them grumpy. Sadly, the worst bully is a great white shark named Clarence. He has been angry since he was a pup. Refer to him only as "C-Fin" if you know what's good for you.

On one particular day, The Sharks and Barry ventured pretty far from the reef and came upon what looked like a rippling, floating island. It extends as far as their fisheyes can see, and C-Fin suggests it warrants investigation. So, The Sharks and Barry swim closer and closer to the island.

I need to interrupt this story for a quick moment to impart some important information to you. The Sharks are much bigger than Barry Cuda and have rows and rows of very sharp teeth—lots more very sharp teeth than Barry Cuda. Sharks can spin and thrash about in the water, roiling the water with immense turbulence. Barry cannot.

Now, where were we? *Ah, yessss*, the rippling, floating island. The closer the Sharks came to the island, the stranger the island became.

Now, I know I have been a bit disparaging when referring to The Sharks' and Barry's mental acuity. However, I would bet there is neither fish nor crab nor shrimp nor turtle nor any denizen of their reef that would have the slightest clue of the origins of this island. But we know, don't we? And so, unknowingly, they swam on. And then, it happened: the plastic bags, six-pack rings, and whatever other waste had joined together in creating a rippling, floating island of trash, seemed to grab at The Sharks and Barry. Then the thrashing and biting began, and... well... The Sharks escaped and swam away, leaving Barry Cuda alone and trapped in the debris. Not a fate any fish would wish on any other fish, even one as shallow as Barry.

The Sharks returned to the reef, and Barry's absence did not go unnoticed. It seems Ophelia was in the habit of keeping tabs on Barry. She knew he had left with The Sharks and saw he had not returned with them.

Bravely, Ophelia swam up to C-Fin, asked about Barry's whereabouts, and got some fishy answers about his leaving the group mid-sea.

Ophelia was devastated – knowing no good could come of this – and started to cry uncontrollably, which did not go unnoticed by Ned because – Oh, you know why.

Ned couldn't stand Ophelia's grief, so, completely flat and completely round, Ned swam from the reef in the direction from which the sharks had come, intent on learning the fate of Barry Cuda. Ned swam and swam. It was pretty brave for a fish who had never left his reef, and after what seemed like hours, he came upon the rippling, floating island... and Barry Cuda.

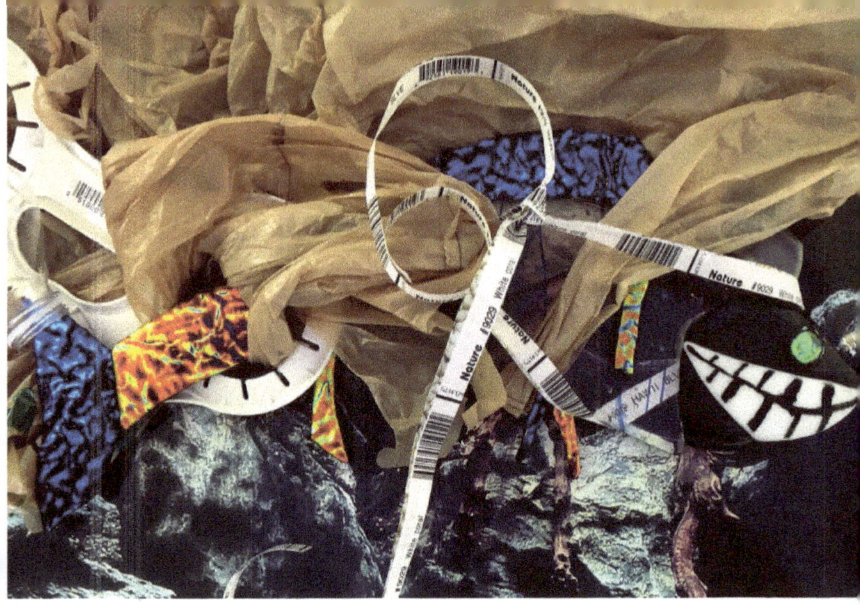

Barry had no fight left in him. He was barely breathing and was extremely exhausted.

Ned was treading water, analyzing the situation, realizing that Barry was wrapped in something like a jellyfish without tentacles – or what we would call plastic bags.

Ned never thought being flat AND round would ever serve any purpose other than announcing to the world that he had uncontrollable emotions. However, it seemed that, in this situation, flat and round was just what he needed to be. Ned swam up to Barry and gently pushed his thin fins between Barry and the "jellyfish" and wiggled and wriggled until he loosened its hold.

He repeated this exercise wherever it seemed Barry was trapped. Ultimately and thankfully, Barry was freed.

It seems that Barry had lots of time for self-reflection while he slowly was becoming part of the rippling, floating island. He determined that his attitude was lousy, that his choices were terrible, and that his past behavior was unacceptable. After he profusely thanked Ned for saving him, Barry and Ned swam back to the reef as friends. Ned was a hero.

I'd like to say that Ophelia was overwhelmed by Ned's courage and realized that he was the fish for her, but she still only had eyes for Barry.

But wait! There's good news – Barry became a better Barry, and he and Ophelia became a lovely couple.

Ned realized that Ophelia was not the only fish in the sea. Besides, after seeing the rippling, floating island first-hand, Ned knew, with the strongest of emotions, that he had to dedicate all his time to saving the sea. So, he is still very flat AND still very round, and he is also very proud of his efforts.